Therapy after Mom Died

Therapy after Mom Died

Unpacking an Extraordinary Mother-Daughter Relationship

Lacey Tezino

Copyright © 2023 by Lacey Tezino.

Library of Congress Control Number:		2023917380
ISBN:	Hardcover	979-8-3694-0726-4
	Softcover	979-8-3694-0727-1
	eBook	979-8-3694-0728-8

All rights reserved. No part of this book may be reproduced or transmitted in any form or by any means, electronic or mechanical, including photocopying, recording, or by any information storage and retrieval system, without permission in writing from the copyright owner.

Any people depicted in stock imagery provided by Getty Images are models, and such images are being used for illustrative purposes only. Certain stock imagery © Getty Images.

Print information available on the last page.

Rev. date: 10/12/2023

To order additional copies of this book, contact:
Xlibris
844-714-8691
www.Xlibris.com
Orders@Xlibris.com
549791

Contents

Introduction vii
Foreword xi
Honor xiii

Session 1:   A Mother's Sacrifice 3
Session 2:   Orphan Vibes 11
Session 3:   Meeting Her 19
Session 4:   Identity 33
Session 5:   Alcohol 43
Session 6:   Dark Thoughts 53
Session 7:   Meeting Him 61
Session 8:   Cancer 71
Session 9:   Her Death 79
Session 10: Our Legacy 87

About the Author 93

Introduction

In 1986, I doubt that it was easy or "normal" for a one-armed, white gay man to adopt a black newborn baby, but they made it work.

My mother lived a chaotic lifestyle, and when she became pregnant with me, she arrived at a profound realization: motherhood wasn't a burden that she wanted to carry again. With another child already brought into this world without a clear plan for his future, adoption became an inescapable destiny for me.

I was given away to a charming stranger whom my mother met behind a bar, a man who vowed to provide me with a good life and a promising future. All things considered, I turned out alright, but I can't help but find the whole situation rather bizarre, especially given the context of the '80s.

I didn't meet my mother until I reached the age of eighteen. We had a wild decade together, and then she died. We deserved more time with one another. I feel cheated, robbed of the moments we could have shared together. In hindsight, I wish I had mourned her differently, honoring her memory in a way that reflected our bond yet embodied graceful acceptance for the gaps.

Some of my coping methods were healthy, and some were reckless. On good days, I traveled to beautiful countries on her wish list and felt her spirit in each one. I journaled about her life on long plane rides and lit candles on her birthday. On the worst days, I would take the remaining anxiety pills and expired pain medication from her cancer treatment, and then chase those pills down with bottles of Jack Daniels. I indulged in unhealthy food, avoided exercise, and physically abandoned myself. I pushed everyone away. Nothing worked—nothing eased the pain.

Experiencing the loss of my mother, for the second time, completely shattered me. It was an unimaginable year of grief. I had experienced five other close deaths in the months leading up to my mother's passing. When Mom received her diagnosis, she said "I don't want to die this year. You'll be too busy grieving everyone else." She was funny like that. Even with her death, she wanted the spotlight.

But just when I felt my lowest, a glimmer of hope emerged. My high school sweetheart reconnected with me through Instagram, and our love story reignited with an intensity that brought me out of the dark. After nine months of long-distance love, I made a life-altering decision to leave my job in the Middle East and return to Houston to build a life together.

Our love felt like a reward after the pain I had endured. He brought a breath of fresh air and taught me that I deserved happiness. It was the most blissful season of my life – a new home, a beautiful wedding, and my first child. However, a few years into our marriage, my unresolved grief for my mother resurfaced in a way I could no longer ignore.

I was crying on my closet floor, with an old sports bra pulled up to my neck and a breastfeeding pump tugging on both breasts when I had a revelation: I needed therapy!

I was terrified of starting therapy.

I wasn't ashamed or embarrassed—I was scared.

A few years later, the world was falling apart, and I finally opened myself up to the idea.

There were countless moments that could have driven me to seek therapy earlier, but I always found reasons to postpone it—cost, time, fear of a mismatch.

It wasn't until the pandemic, with me confined at home alongside two young children, my husband working remotely, and my eighty-year-old grandmother, that I finally took the plunge. I reached out to a trusted friend and asked for her recommendation for the best therapist in Houston. She nailed it!

My therapist was Elise, and this book chronicles ten of our sessions that helped me navigate the complexities of my mother's life, our relationship, and her untimely passing.

With these sessions, Mom's existence felt real again. Her impact is deeply permanent. Her influence etched itself deeply into my being, evident in my recollection of cherished moments, significant days, and invaluable life lessons.

I've leaned into the honor of my role as a daughter—her daughter. She wasn't flawless, but she was more powerful than any human I have encountered.

This book is a vessel for my grief and love to transcend from my world into yours.

My sincere hope is that if you find even a hint of familiarity in these sessions, you will feel less alone.

Approach it with care, relate to what you can, and savor the journey.

Foreword

My friend Bettie DeBruhl often spoke about her daughter, Lacey, with such pride that I couldn't imagine that they had not spent a lifetime together.

I first met Lacey in the final days of Bettie's life, as cancer took over her body in hospice. The baby girl whom Bettie had given up for adoption stood before me, looking just like her mother—beautiful and tall with deep brown eyes. Bettie had told me years earlier how she was reunited with Lacey, then a college student, and how they formed a bond over a decade.

Motherhood was not easy for Bettie because she was so unusual. Her life was a world without boundaries. As a friend and mother, she was never confined by what society thought or what anyone thought, really. Most of us need rules or a code to live by, but Bettie did not. She didn't give a damn either, and she had a sense of humor about it.

Despite her shortcomings, Bettie was a life force that many of us marveled at, secretly hoping that a pinch of her intoxicating energy would rub off like fairy dust.

I met Bettie more than twenty years ago, and we quickly became friends. Kindred Capricorns who worked hard and loved life. We had a mutual respect for how we moved through the world. Perhaps I gave her a sense of stability because of my family roots. She gave me herself—flaws and all. She was a savvy public relations strategist with an incredible talent for details who also could be the person dancing on bar tables at closing and going home with a friend's boyfriend.

Without rules and boundaries to tether herself to, Bettie's life was messy, and so was motherhood. She never apologized for it, but she was never mean about it either. I respected her for that.

Our friendship over the years was often strained by Bettie's unbounded life, which impinged on my boundaries, but my love for her as a friend never waned.

While in hospice, Bettie pulled me close and asked me if she was going to die.

"There's too much hell for you to raise on Earth to die right now," I whispered.

She laughed.

I know she tried as much as she was capable to be Lacey's mother. Despite her tragically flawed life, Bettie Debruhl loved her daughter, and Lacey loved her back.

This is their remarkable story.

Joy Sewing

Honor

My Bettie,
It was an incredible honor to be your daughter.

Sweet Ziggy,
It is my greatest joy to be your mother.

Session 1

A Mother's Sacrifice

My first therapy session was a shit show. It was supposed to be a relaxed ninety-minute intake appointment, a simple opportunity for the therapist to get to know me. However, of those ninety minutes, I spent eighty-nine in tears. My computer initiated an update right before the session, so I frantically scrambled to join the call. Strangely, this still felt easier than driving across town and sitting in a cold waiting room. I was beyond nervous. Participating in my very first session from the comfort of my bedroom allowed me to unravel in my own private space.

Elise was my therapist. She was beauty pageant beautiful. She had an impeccable background scene of her home office and makeup that was perfectly glowing. I had a lump in my throat before saying a word.

"Hi, Lacey, it's so nice to meet you," Elise said with a warm smile that felt more authentic than I expected through a computer screen.

As I opened my mouth to return the pleasant greeting, I burst into tears. I covered my face to mute the sob.

Elise rubbed her hand over her chest in a slow circular motion. Her face made a small pout that made me melt further. She was patient and had no problem with silence. I have always been uncomfortable with long pauses while staring at another human, so I urged us forward.

Through my tears, "I guess I should tell you why I am here, right?"

Elise assured me that this initial session would be comfortable and tailored to my pace. Together, we would establish a baseline of where I was and set goals for where I wanted to go. I shared that my primary motivation for seeking therapy stemmed from the persistent regrets tied to my relationship with my mother and her passing, which constantly weighed on my mind.

Elise nodded thoughtfully, "We'll start from the beginning. Tell me about both of your parents."

I just started rambling and recalling the details as honestly and as scattered as I knew them.

* * *

My birth certificate lists Ronald Huckaby as my father, whom I knew as Ronnie, and Elizabeth DeBruhl, whom I knew as Bettie, as my mother. Surprisingly, both have white designated as their race. I wonder how that was allowed. Photos from my birth show Bettie lying in bed, her beautifully tanned skin contrasting with a large, frizzy afro. It must have been clear to the hospital staff that she wasn't white.

I imagine that both of their identities and desires complicated the adoption. Ronnie did not have a partner; same sex marriage was not yet legal, and he willingly accepted this parental journey as a single father. Bettie was clear that she wanted to release her maternal rights before I was ever born.

I took a breath and paused to explain to Elise that I didn't get the full and accurate story of my parents until adulthood.

Growing up, Ronnie's family told me that my mother was a drug addict and that she gave me up at birth. Also, I was told that she was dead and that either HIV or drug use had killed her. It was confusing to be told that my mother was dead, but that no one knew the cause. I was made to believe that Bettie and Ronnie were romantically involved, but never married. Long story short, I understood that he wanted to keep me, but she did not, and that was the reason they separated. If anyone ever asked, I was to tell them that my mother was Hawaiian and that my father was white.

There were so many lies. Well, Ronnie was white—that was true—but he wasn't my biological father. Bettie was Samoan, not Hawaiian. They were never dating or involved. It was simply an arrangement. My mother gave me away—that was the arrangement.

The truth was that my biological father, Sonny, met Bettie during her wild party days. They fell for one another, and he decided that he wanted to be a truck driver. Sonny invited my mother to keep him company in the passenger seat across the country. After a few weeks on the road, she became pregnant. Instead of telling Sonny about the pregnancy, she called her sister and begged for a plane ticket to Houston, leaving him clueless in California. She wasn't planning to keep me, so she decided that Sonny was better off without the news.

My mom landed in Houston and headed to find comfort. She was a regular in the bar that Ronnie owned. Through the startling news of another baby, the solution had to be at the bottom of a vodka martini. After a few glasses, her typical routine was to begin spilling her life's regrets to anyone that would listen. Ronnie would lean over the bar and entertain her drunken revelations with empathy and free counseling. However, this day was special.

"I'm pregnant," Mom confessed. "I can't keep this baby. I can't even take care of the son that I have now."

My mother admitted that she was planning an abortion. She had several abortions in her past and felt that this was the obvious next step.

Ronnie was shocked by her blunt confession, yet he found himself intrigued by her dilemma. For years, he had suppressed his desire to have a baby but couldn't think of anything he wanted more. He knew being gay wouldn't allow the start of his family to happen naturally. He'd contemplated adoption but also knew that it would take an unconventional agreement to make it possible.

In the midst of her confession, he exclaimed, "Let me have your baby!"

His request, though impulsive, was straightforward and genuine. While she initially found it absurd, Mom was curious to learn more about his intentions. She looked Ronnie up and down - with his t-shirt tied off at the shoulder, one arm missing, and his free hand resting on the bar. Could she really give her child away to this one-armed, white gay man?

Ronnie wanted to wait until she was sober to talk about real options, so they agreed to meet for lunch the next day. In a small café, just down the street from the bar, Ronnie anxiously waited for thirty minutes. Just as he thought she had changed her mind and decided not to show, Bettie entered, shuffling through the door in an oversized University of Houston sweater, dark sunglasses, and white Converse high tops. Despite her killer hangover, she managed to recall their previous conversation. Ronnie was prepared to discuss the plan. He explained his long desire to become a father and made sure that his pure intentions came through during the conversation. Ronnie proposed placing Bettie into a rehabilitation facility called The Shoulder and requested she remain sober for the remainder of her pregnancy. He promised to deliver food and any toiletries that she needed directly to the facility.

Mom wasn't thrilled about the rehab request, but she figured that would give her some time to clear her head. First, she had to spend some time in jail for a "failure to appear" charge in court. She served her time, and there were only a few days left until she was scheduled for check in at The Shoulder.

Just a month before my birth, Dad enlisted the help of a lawyer friend who agreed to spearhead the legal adoption paperwork. My mother willingly surrendered all her parental rights.

The arrangement was formalized, and the adoption became final in June 1986. Shortly after, my mother was diagnosed with HIV, which was then seen as a death sentence. She offered Ronnie the option to back out of their agreement, but he didn't budge. Ronnie went above and beyond to ensure a healthy final month of pregnancy, taking care of her needs and fulfilling his part of the agreement.

I was born on July 28, 1986. I can't comprehend the emotions that my mother wrestled with while nearing my birth. She must have suffered normal bits of anxiety while silently accepting that she wouldn't be taking me home from the hospital.

My dad allowed her to spend the first night with me, but the next morning, I was packed up and brought to his home. That was it. Mom didn't see me again until I showed up on her doorstep eighteen years later.

When I met my mother, I asked her how she felt the day I was born, and her eyes began to water. She said that it was the hardest decision that she had ever made. She never regretted her choice, which made me feel slighted, but I understood later that it was the right move.

According to my family, she popped up after the delivery and immediately left the hospital. But her version is far different: In it, she held me close and rocked me all night. She told me about the emotional night that she'd spent in the nursery, connecting with me those first few hours of my life, and I believe her. I feel like those few hours established a connection that would linger in her heart until we finally met again.

For some reason, hearing my mother's side of the birth story changed my view of her and myself. Hearing that I was worthy of her love, even if it was only for one night, felt good. I have struggled my whole life with being grateful to those that took care of me and resentful for the one who didn't. I couldn't help but to fall in love with my mom when I met her. I still had resentful moments, but she was incredibly resilient, and I was proud to be her daughter.

My mother did not give me up easily—it involved her going to rehab, making the hard choices, getting her life together, and sacrificing the life she enjoyed — all to secure my chance at a relatively unscathed future. My mother confided in her closest friends, heard criticism from her family, and in unanimous agreement, they all recognized that the timing wasn't right for her to raise another child.

I'm torn between viewing adoption as a gesture of both selflessness and selfishness, but then I realize that maybe it's perfectly acceptable for it to be both. I came to accept that my mother was probably a blend of both.

* * *

"What a beautiful way into this world," Elise added as I wrapped up my adoption story.

Elise made me feel seen. I have told this story many times before, but this time was different.

Elise took in my story and held it gently while I cried. She made notes, gave warm smiles, and wrapped up our time by thanking me for trusting her.

I let out a sigh of relief and said, "I'll see you next week!"

Session 2

Orphan Vibes

I was officially one of those "my-therapist-said" women, and I wore it like a badge of honor.

With just one session under my belt, I couldn't wait for our next appointment to roll around. I managed to tell everyone who would listen that I was in therapy. I felt proud and wanted the world to know that I was on a journey to self-improvement.

Elise beat me to our second session. I had scheduled it during my lunch break at work, but the prior meeting ran late. Looking back, I don't know why I thought cramming therapy into my workday was a wise decision, especially after the excessive tears from our first meeting. At that point, I was only a few months postpartum, and my hormones remained tangled and unrecognizable.

I joined the session a bit flustered, and there she was—calm and smiling. I immediately sank into my chair and felt relief.

I vented about work for the first few minutes, and she let me go at it.

When I took a breath from the work drama, she slipped in a reminder of the goals we set during session one.

"I know you would like to stay within ten sessions and work through unresolved feelings about your mom."

The directness jolted me a little bit, but then I appreciated that she was bringing accountability to the relationship.

"Let's talk about you growing up without your mom. How was your childhood?" Elise asked.

* * *

Growing up without a mother sucks. Even though I was surrounded by some of the most caring people in the world, that didn't erase the fact nor feelings that accompany being an orphan: a child deprived by death of one or usually both parents.

My father began raising me as a single parent and hired a full-time nanny from Mexico. My family recalls my first language being Spanish, which indicates to me that this nanny played a huge role in my infancy. I don't remember her, but I feel grateful to this woman. I sometimes wonder if she is still alive out there and if she remembers caring for me. Did she have kids? Did she have a daughter? Did she treat me like her own daughter?

When I was nearly two years old, Ronnie's cancer unexpectedly returned, and our only option was to move back to his hometown with his family. We required assistance with daily care, both for me and to manage his symptoms. That's how it happened. That's how a black eighteen-month-old girl and a twenty-nine-year-old white gay father found themselves in Vidor, Texas. It was an unexpected move for our non-traditional family, but it was essential. We needed to be near family.

Ronnie was a dream of a father. He read me bedtime stories every night, sometimes gave me ice cream for breakfast, and took me on enchanting berry-picking adventures. His undivided attention meant the world to me. I vividly remember gazing up at his towering figure with my innocent eyes, marveling at his strength and determination, despite his missing arm. I loved my father and feel that he is the reason that I love those around me with such tenderness.

Although kids are typically grossly unprepared for a parent's death, I knew it was coming. Cancer kills people and I knew it was going to take my dad. I was clear that though he had beat it before, this time was different. Ronnie and his mom would routinely drive to Houston for scans to confirm that the cancer did not come back to his lungs or chest area, but they never checked any other part of his body. Unsuspectingly, we discovered that tumors were growing in his brain, and by the time they were found, his days were already dwindling.

My dad went to the hospital for the last time on a Sunday, and he died the following Thursday. My grandmother recalls the helplessness of those final days, and anyone who has ever embarked on the journey toward the end of life, or ridden the morphine train, understands the blurry waiting game that ends in heartache. My grandmother said he pushed the button for as much morphine as possible and that he passed without pain. I can't imagine the feeling of watching your child leave the world right before your eyes.

Lillian Huckaby was the one person who made my parental void bearable. I knew that she wasn't my mother; I called her Nana, just like all the other kids in the family. But one day, when I was about ten years old, I mustered the courage to ask her if it would be okay to call her Mom. Her smile was the most comforting and understanding thing in this world. I tried it for a day, but it felt so weird. We didn't discuss it, and I never addressed her as such again. She was firm, yet graceful when I asked her questions about my real mother. She never meant any harm with her responses. To the best of her knowledge, my mother had HIV, and in the '80s, people with the disease often didn't live healthy lives, if they survived at all. She would gently tell me that my mother had passed away when I was young. As I grew older, her responses became more detailed, painting a picture of my mother's struggles with drug addiction and a tumultuous lifestyle. In hindsight, I feel a deep sympathy for my grandmother. Raising me without real answers couldn't have been easy.

At my father's funeral, people talked as if I couldn't hear or understand them. People would whisper over my head, forming earmuffs with their hands, "How is she doing with all of this?" I felt numb, convinced that no one in this room understood my pain and emptiness. That selfish feeling quickly dissolved when I walked to the front row and saw the look on my grandmother's face. Her tears were dry and crusted against her emotionless face. She was staring at the casket in a daze. Her hands clutched tightly onto her tissues, legs crossed underneath the bench, shaking in a fast motion. I gently placed my little fingers on her leg and kept my head down to avoid direct eye contact. That's when she broke. She wrapped her arms around my entire body and began weeping so loud that I still remember the exact pitch. In that moment, I realized something profound: she was hurting more than me. This was how a mother feels when they lose their child. From that day forward, I believed that my grandmother's love for her son had been transferred directly to me.

At that point, I was a real orphan. To my knowledge, my mother and father were both gone.

I carried an embarrassment of not having parents, concocting elaborate stories to make their lives seem more interesting. I took small details I had heard from my family and spun them into extravagant lies.

I'll never forget the time I shared the most unbelievable story during a sleepover with my cheerleading squad. I had already told them my mom was from Hawaii and they wanted more details about her. Since I didn't have any real stories, I told them that she died at birth because they were delivering me in a remote village in Hawaii where they used sticks to pull babies out. How ridiculous it all sounds now!

* * *

I hadn't thought about that story until this day with Elise. My cheeks turned a little red just recalling the details of my lie.

We concluded the session, both acknowledging the undeniable difficulty of growing up without a mother. Still, I knew in my heart that having a grandmother like mine had been my saving grace.

As we wrapped up, Elise inquired, "You mentioned your grandmother now lives with you, is that right?"

I couldn't help but smile as I recounted the story. "My house is a bit of a chaotic circus. After a devastating hurricane hit Texas, my grandmother's house was flooded. She never wanted to leave her home and hoped that moving in with us would be temporary. But after two months under our roof, she came to me with tears in her eyes and said, 'If I'm not a burden here, I'd like to live with you permanently.' I hugged her tighter than ever before, assuring her that I would take care of her and that she was always welcome in my home."

Our time was up, and Elise expressed her amazement, saying, "You are wonderful, Lacey. You chose to take care of your grandmother, just as she did for you."

My voice trembled with emotion as I offered my final words before ending the call, "She was my mother when I didn't have one. I owe her my life."

Session 3

Meeting Her

I was counting down the days until my next appointment!

All week, I had thought about seeing Elise and telling her the story about how I met my mom. She now knew about the adoption and growing up without my mother. It was time to share how we met.

I pulled into an empty parking lot to attend our session from my phone. We didn't waste any time at all. I think she could see my anticipation through the screen.

"I'm ready to hear about meeting your mom for the first time. How did that happen?" Elise asked.

***

My voice trembled and my hands were shaking, "I believe I'm your daughter." It was the first time I had ever heard my mother's voice. On this day, I shattered the belief I had held for eighteen long years – the belief that I was an orphan.

The morning that I met my mother for the first time was hectic. I was startled awake by my 5:30 a.m. alarm clock. I needed to be at the HEB gas station to open the shift at 6:00 a.m. Oh, how I wanted so badly to call in sick! I had been out drinking all night, and my brain literally felt like it was sitting on my skull. I needed water, a greasy egg McMuffin and big fountain coke. I fell back asleep for ten more minutes; therefore, I didn't get any of those things that I needed.

I dashed out the door without a shower, the lingering scent of cheap vodka clinging to me like a ten-dollar cologne. In five frantic minutes, I was out the door. As soon as I reached my car, the hangover plunged into overdrive. I had to run back inside and at least get the blue Gatorade from the refrigerator door. I was at the stoplight next to my job at 5:56 AM, and I knew I wouldn't be clocking in on time. I had already been late for the same 6:00 a.m. shift the week before, so I knew that my supervisor was going to have a fit.

Screeching into the parking lot, I saw her pull up alongside me. Oddly, she seemed to be in an unusually good mood, whistling and chuckling as she approached the store's entrance.

"We almost didn't make it!" she exclaimed with a grin.

We unlocked the door and began turning on all the lights of the grocery store. Just as I had grabbed the keys to the gas station kiosk outside, she shouted over, asking if I had plans to surprise my mother after work. After eighteen years, you'd think I'd have mastered a better response to Mother's Day queries, but I blurted back, "Nope, I don't have a mom!" Walking out of the grocery store and toward the kiosk, I felt my face flush and a lump forming in my throat. It was too early to be this sensitive. I could have been better about my response back there.

I unlocked the back door, slipped into my usual chair, and began to sort the cash in the register. My mind, however, drifted to my usual Mother's Day blues. Around 8 a.m., with just two customers to occupy my time, I suddenly remembered a family tree assignment due for my English composition course.

I ran my fingers over the face of my phone and wondered if I was serious about this attempt, this desire to find out more about my birth mother. Before I could chicken out, I dialed 1411 and requested a residential number listing in Houston, Texas. I provided the name listed on my birth certificate and the operator set about her search.

"I've found two listings under that name," she reported. I was taken aback but excited that these numbers might lead me to information about my mother.

My palms grew sweaty, and my mouth turned dry as I waited. Just as my nerves peaked, a man tapped on the gas station kiosk's glass window, startling me. My phone tumbled to the ground, and I fumbled to pick it up. Desperate to find someone still willing to help, I stammered a hello twice. Then, after an agonizing pause, the most beautiful voice I had ever heard graced the line.

I swallowed the boulder sized lump in my throat and asked if I could speak to Elizabeth.

She calmly replied, "Yes, that's me. May I ask who is calling?"

I had my eyes closed and squinting as hard as I could, as if I was waiting for some type of explosion. My lips were pressed together tightly, and I blurted out, "I think I'm your daughter, La—"

Before I could finish my full name, "Lacey! Yes, Lacey!" I heard her take a deep breath, sort of like an aggressive gasp.

"I'm so sorry for calling this early." My eyes immediately filled with tears. I melted into the chair and held my cell phone with both hands against my ear.

"No, sweetie, don't be." Mom reassured me. Her voice carried the shock and excitement she felt, all while maintaining a soothing calmness for my sake.

Just as she began to ask where I was, I looked up to see a line of four people waiting to pay for their gas.

"Okay, look, I'm really sorry. I am at work right now and will have to call you on my break." I quickly extended the cash drawer out to the next customer and gave a nervous smile as I wasn't sure how long he had been waiting.

"Please don't hang up," Mom pleaded. I knew that this was such bad timing and a crazy introduction to Mother's Day morning, but I promised to call back within the hour.

My mind was racing, heart pounding, and a huge grin stretched across my face. It was her. She was my mom. She was real. I finished serving the remaining customers and became extremely anxious to call her back. I decided that I wouldn't tell my family until after the meeting. It wasn't so much that I wanted to be secretive. I just didn't want them to worry about me.

With sweaty palms and a racing heart, I dialed her number once more. She asked where I was now, and I told her that I lived in Huntsville, Texas, attending college. It was merely an hour's drive from her apartment in Houston.

"Come tonight. I'll cook dinner!" She was so excited that I couldn't turn down the offer. I agreed, and we swiftly worked out the details of timing and location. In less than two hours, I would be off. What should I wear? Should I bring a gift? I figured that I could stop inside of the grocery store for flowers on my way out. Finally, 2:00 p.m. arrived. I clocked out and picked out the best-looking bouquet.

As I was paying at the register, my supervisor stopped me with a confused look. "Did you make plans with some friends?" she asked.

With a big smile, "Nope. I am going to meet my mom for the first time." I can imagine how strange this was, after my reaction this morning, but she smiled and gave me a big hug.

I rushed home to shower and change, sharing the news with my roommate, Guinevere, who listened attentively to my worries and doubts. She offered to ride with me, but I decided that I should go alone.

I didn't want to overdress, yet I also didn't want to appear super casual. I decided on jeans, a pink-striped button-up shirt, and a black vest. I straightened a few of the back pieces of my hair and then just pulled the sides half up with bobby pins. I didn't want to waste time that we could be spending together, so I was out the door within forty-five minutes.

I plugged her address into the GPS, and I was on my way. Even with the hangover, this day had me so excited and nervous that I couldn't eat anything. I quickly stopped by for some cheese Doritos and a Sprite to avoid getting to the dinner table starving, but I couldn't stomach it. I had never been this nervous in my life. My hands shook on the steering wheel. I had to keep the wind blowing cold in my face.

The GPS read two minutes to the destination, and I felt like I was going to be sick. I had to pull over immediately. The few chips I had managed to eat now lay by the side of the road. Struggling to catch my breath, I leaned against the open car door, grateful for the small side street before her building. I rinsed my mouth with Sprite and peered at my reflection in the visor mirror.

"Come on, Lacey. You can do this!" I had to coach myself.

I sunk into the gravity of the situation. My head was spinning with thoughts of this being the last day that I didn't have a mom. I had so many dreams about who she would be and how we would bond. Ready or not—it was time.

I took a deep breath and the phone rang. Her sweet voice asked, "Hey, are you doing okay? What is your ETA?" I explained that I was pulling into the complex now.

What the hell am I doing? That was my final thought before meeting my mom.

She provided the gate code, and as I pulled into the first level of the garage, I saw her son walk out first. I whispered to myself, "That's my brother." He had a strange-looking girl following behind him with an oversized T-shirt that was falling off her shoulder. I wondered who she was, but also didn't care. Charles, my mom's boyfriend, was directly behind them. As my brother waved me into a visitor parking spot, I caught a glimpse of my mother for the first time. I took a deep breath, grabbed the bouquet of flowers, and stepped out of my car.

She approached with a striking presence that I can still recall to this day. Her attire was casual yet captivating: a crimson button-up shirt that reached just past her mid-thigh, paired with dark blue jeans and sandals. Her thick curls were tamed into a sleek ponytail, framing her beautiful face. Our eyes locked as she neared, and we both covered our mouths, drawing closer until we embraced wholeheartedly. Time seemed to stand still. The gentle pressure of her arm around my neck, the scent of her that I had longed for, and the soft sobs that resonated in my ear as our chests pressed tightly together — it was the most beautiful moment of my life. She was stunning, and we both deserved this moment.

As we slowly parted, we wiped away the tears that had welled up. Though I was still trembling with emotion, I mustered the courage to embrace my brother. His presence felt familiar, and instantly we had an indescribable connection.

The family moment was enchanting, and I selfishly reveled in the emotions, momentarily neglecting to properly acknowledge my brother's awkward girlfriend. Charles had tears in his eyes too. He and my mother had been dating for several years, and the significance of this moment overwhelmed him.

We engaged in small talk about the traffic and the weather as we made our way to the elevator and ascended to their apartment.

Therapy after Mom Died

It was tastefully decorated with hints of modern art, exuding an inviting sense of luxury. A sumptuous meal was spread across the table, filling the room with a mouthwatering smell. My mother, it seemed, cooked like one of those magazine women with everything perfectly plated. Despite the delectable food, a queasy feeling still churned in my stomach.

As we sat down to eat, there was an undeniable tension in the air, owing to the nervousness of two strong-willed women who were feeling somewhat shy.

Later in life, those who met us would often remark that when we were together, we seemed to consume all the oxygen in the room, leaving only a small share for others. Although it might have been a backhanded compliment, I took it as a testament to our boldness and captivating presence.

Damien uncorked the first bottle of wine, and this brought a quick ease to the room. After the third glass, we were all feeling relaxed and spilling out old memories and things about each other. As I sat there, engrossed in our conversation, my mother casually dropped the names "Ronnie" and "your dad" multiple times, each referring to distinct individuals. It took her a little while to notice the puzzled look and furrow in my brow, a silent plea for clarification.

Finally, unable to ignore my confusion any longer, she hesitated before gently revealing, "You do know that Ronnie wasn't your biological father, right?" The room suddenly plunged into a heavy silence, and I found myself struggling to swallow the bold, red wine that lingered in my mouth.

I managed to stammer out, "Hmm, I did not know that." My mother, seemingly overwhelmed by a mix of regret and sorrow, covered her face with her hands and burst into tears.

Amidst her sobs, she managed to explain, "You see, he was gay, and he wanted a child, but it was difficult. I was planning to have an abortion. We had an agreement." Her words hung in the air, heavy with the gravity of the secret she had carried for so long. She felt torn, as though it wasn't her place to disclose this truth, yet also believed it was a disservice that I had remained in the dark all this time.

We went to the patio and sat for hours. They wanted to hear stories about me growing up in Vidor, and I was eager to hear stories about their lives together. Considering how Mom was living now, I would have never guessed that she was the same woman that my family had portrayed as "A heavy drug addict who couldn't handle a baby." I had this one photo of her and my dad holding me on the day I was born. I used to keep it in a locked jewelry box under my bed. When I got sad, I would look at the picture and kiss her. She was the most beautiful woman I had ever seen. Even meeting her at forty-three, she was still gorgeous! She lived in a nice area of Houston, drove a Lexus SUV, and was looking to buy a house with her recent promotion to an executive role at the PR agency where she worked. She didn't fit the image my family had painted all these years.

The wine allowed me to be extremely blunt with my questioning. I asked her how she changed her life so drastically. I asked her about her reasons for agreeing to the adoption. The more I dug, the more emotional we became. She apologized nearly twenty times that night. She felt terrible that I ended up in Vidor, Texas. Charles, who was an intelligent black activist, had much to say and ask about my upbringing. I was offended by his questioning at first, but then it felt oddly protective and comforting. He recounted his experience coming to Vidor to find me. He took a huge risk by visiting my home a few years prior, but he couldn't ignore his curiosity. When he arrived, he lied about who he was and caused a big storm with my family. Mom recounted how she had asked him multiple times not to approach me at such a young age. Truth be told, I just think that she wasn't ready.

After sharing stories about Ronnie, I was overcome with emotion, finally understanding his love for me. How extraordinary must he have been to decide that he wanted me? Despite his health, his sexual orientation, my mother's HIV, and even the fact that he would have a black baby — he wanted me more than anything else in the world. I could never honor him as much as he deserved. My mom cried as I poured out my heart, expressing how much I missed him.

It grew late in the evening, so my brother brought out blankets from the closet and set up the sofa for me. He made a small pallet on the floor for himself, and we both passed out before Mom and Charles could finish cleaning the kitchen.

I had an 8:00 a.m. class the following morning. I woke up, utterly dehydrated and slightly dizzy, around five. Everyone was still asleep. Quietly, I used the restroom and gathered my things to leave. It felt like an awkward one-night stand. I looked around the kitchen for a piece of paper and a pen and did the only appropriate thing I could think of — I wrote a note.

> "Thank you for our amazing first date. You were just as I dreamed and more. Forgive me if things get a little weird after this. I have many things to process and a whole life of lies to reconcile. No matter what, we must move forward. It was very nice to meet you."
> Love,
> Lacey

My brother rolled over just as I cracked the front door. He opened his eyes and smiled. I returned a half-smile and waved. "I'll see you soon!"

I got in my car and sat there for ten minutes, trying to piece together the details from the night before. My dominant emotion was anger. My family had lied to me, and I felt foolish. I wasn't sure how I was going to broach the subject with them.

As I began to drive away, I decided to call my cousin Cody. I woke him out of his sleep, and he couldn't comprehend my greeting. "You will never believe who I met last night!"

He sounded a little annoyed, questioning if I were dying and why I would be calling this early.

"I met my mom last night. I am in Houston, Texas. She is alive. She is alive! My dad was gay. I was adopted." I rushed through the details, my voice cracking as I tried to cram everything into that brief moment. There was a long pause.

"We were always told not to tell you." I couldn't believe his response. Thinking I heard him wrong; I asked him to repeat it. "Lacey, don't hate us. We just wanted to protect you."

* * *

I noticed Elise's eyes drift to the bottom corner of her screen, a subtle yet unmistakable sign that our allotted hour had come to an end.

Throughout the session, I had barely taken a moment to catch my breath, pouring my heart into the memory my mother's discovery. We were now a few minutes beyond the scheduled cutoff time, and I sensed the need to break the silence, allowing Elise to attend to her next client.

I cleared my throat, attempting to downplay the emotional weight of my narrative. "It's a wild story, I know, but I'm okay." My voice wavered, betraying the stoic facade I was trying to maintain.

But Elise wasn't about to let me off the hook that easily. Instead, she leaned in, her voice filled with empathy, and acknowledged the immense courage it took to share such those profound moments from my life. She understood the sheer difficulty of those pivotal moments, and for the first time in a long while, I felt truly heard and understood.

"I feel honored to know you and to have heard this incredible story of reuniting with your mother. Your spirit radiates with resilience," Elise remarked.

With tears in my eyes, I felt a sense of relief, "Thank you for allowing me to share. I'll see you soon."

Session 4

Identity

Just before our session, I grabbed a vanilla protein shake, although what I really craved was a bag of Cheetos.

I have struggled with my weight my whole life. I was always bigger than most girls around me. I envied skinny girls then and envy fit women now.

Elise was one of those fit women. I stalked her social media and quickly realized that she might not be the ideal person to unpack my weight and self-esteem issues with. It wasn't fair for me to dig through all her social media pages, but I wondered if she had done the same with me. Did she analyze my emo captions and long rants, or did she strictly focus on the content of our sessions?

As Elise joined our virtual session, she immediately recognized the brand of protein shake I was sipping. "I love those," she commented with a smile.

"I hate them! I'd take a milkshake any day," I replied, and we shared a laugh. In that moment, my trust in her deepened, prompting me to reconsider sharing the self-confidence issues that had been at the forefront of my mind.

With a deep breath, I began to confide in Elise about the weight I had gained during pregnancy and how it was affecting my self-image. "My mom struggled a lot with her weight. Being Samoan and black doesn't lend itself to a petite frame," I said while acknowledging the influence of genetics on my body type. I tried to brush off my words with a forced laugh, but it fell flat.

Feeling a sense of pride that I knew a clear direction for our session, I said, "I'd like to talk about race a bit today. It's been a gray area for most of my life."

Elise, ever perceptive, gently steered the conversation in the direction I suggested. "Let's explore your identity today. Do you think your self-image is intertwined with your mother's experiences?"

* * *

When I first laid eyes on my mother, I couldn't help but be struck by her exotic beauty. Her features seemed both familiar and enigmatic, not easily categorized into any single ethnic group.

Meeting my mother, my hope was to finally unearth my identity through her. I was naive to believe that all my unsettled feelings of being mixed race would vanish when I met her. I longed to find culture and belonging through my mom, but the truth was she was still searching for that herself.

I asked Mom about her ethnicity one day. The same way white people would ask me while growing up, "What are you?"

This question had the weight of nineteen years of ambiguity riding on it, but somehow it rolled off my tongue as casually as I intended. No pressure. She paused, her expression a mix of uncertainty and insecurity.

"I'm black," she said, without making eye contact. "Haven't you heard of the one-drop rule?" Her words seemed as though she was trying to convince herself as much as she was trying to explain it to me.

Later, I would learn that my mother wasn't entirely certain if the father she adored and wanted so desperately to be her own biological parent was indeed her biological father. She would proudly recount stories of him as one of the most badass men in Washington, DC, almost like a real-life gangster from the movies. He had taken care of her and her siblings after their mother had passed away.

A single photograph of my grandmother, her mother, was all I had. My mother had inherited many features from her, making her look unique in ways that had always enamored me. My mother stood tall at six feet one inch, her long wavy hair cascading down her back. Her lips were full and beautiful, her chin adorned with a mole that nestled in the traditional dimple space. Her brown eyes were strikingly large, brimming with curiosity, and she sported a slight gap between her front teeth. Her eyebrows were impeccably groomed, reminiscent of magazine cover models.

Silver jewelry, especially thin hoop earrings, were her signature. She wore an oversized watch on her left wrist, along with a statement bracelet and several delicate bangles on her right wrist. She often changed her tribal necklaces, each one carrying am interesting backstory.

"Never leave the house without earrings and a nice lipstick," Mom would say, watching me prance around life with little enthusiasm to be fashionable or looking put-together. Whether she was going to the gym or out to a restaurant, she would apply her mantra and cut her eyes at me when I would join her looking a hot mess.

With all her beauty and style, I truly struggled to find relief or refuge within my blurred identity. I didn't feel that my unsophisticated look could possibly come from her and felt even more confused about where I belonged. I expected that finding my mom was going to feel like home, that she was my home. I was disappointed by the lack of my eureka moment with her.

Although Mom proclaimed her blackness and had a black Muslim boyfriend who gave off Malcom X militant vibes—I didn't experience her as a quintessential black woman. I observed her as if I was walking through an art gallery, looking at each piece and realizing that she was up for interpretation.

My mother was incredibly intelligent and well-traveled, resulting in her broad worldview and admiration for all cultures. She had visible and audible disdain for the audacity of white men and women who displayed discrimination. It took her years to fully let the idea sink in that I was raised in Vidor, Texas.

Vidor has a longstanding reputation of being a "sundown" town, where black people are not allowed safely after dark. Even though not all its residents shared the same hatred as Vidor's past, in the 1980s—it was an unusual place for a black girl to grow up.

When I moved into my grandparents' home, the family had a black dog who was named Nigger. The word rolled off everyone's tongue so casually and frequently around me. Despite being told that I wasn't black, the word had a strange and unexplainable impact on me. At the time, I didn't quite understand why, but the word made me cringe and feel so uneasy. I felt afraid at times, although I couldn't articulate it well because I wasn't in any physical danger.

I was an anomaly and for my family, friends, and community—I was known as an exception. Racism wasn't considered disgusting in Vidor; it was almost a birthright. I didn't belong there, but I tried my best to fit in, despite knowing that I was different. My family went to great lengths to shield me from the hatred of a few outspoken bigots who occasionally challenged my ethnicity in ignorant ways.

Girls often stared at my features, got their fingers stuck in my thick hair, and tried on different lipsticks and puckered their lips with attempts to match me. Boys weren't attracted to me, and the ones that were would never get their families' approval, so I was always treated like "just another one of the boys." I had one boyfriend in high school who was brave enough to challenge his families' racist views of me.

Out of all things, my hair was the biggest enemy I had while trying to blend in. It was one of the most conspicuous features that set me apart in my predominantly white surroundings.

My mom had beautiful, thick, and silky hair that I immediately envied when I met her. She asked me, "Who took care of your hair while you were growing up?" Several people had tried, but it was mostly my Aunt Rena who French-braided it on Sundays. I recalled the huge bottles of Mane 'n Tail that my aunt used on my hair, and my mom seemed genuinely interested in hearing more about my hair journey.

I explained that when I reached middle school, my grandmother heard about a black beauty shop in the neighboring town of Beaumont, Texas, where there was a significant African American population.

"I never really liked my hair right after leaving the beauty shop," I admitted. "Inside the shop, while I sat in the chair, they'd spin me around to face the mirror, and I'd smile. All the women around me would give me compliments, and I felt incredibly beautiful with my straightened, smooth hair flowing down my back. Sometimes, I'd sneak and watch black movies on TV when no one else was around. I remember the first time I saw Vanessa Williams, I fell in love. Looking at my freshly pressed hair in the mirror, I would imagine myself as a beautiful black movie star."

My mother listened attentively, her eyes lighting up. "Those salon ladies are like personal hype women!" she exclaimed, and we shared a laugh.

I continued, "There was a sweet older woman who styled my hair each time. She had a gentle way about her and wore dark-rimmed glasses that perched at the tip of her nose. Her name was Ms. Gladys, and her warmth provided me with a sense of comfort that ran deep. She always gave me a hug and asked about my grandma. I'd walk out of the salon with a handful of M&Ms from the candy machine, feeling on top of the world. But as soon as I stepped outside, I was back in my own reality. I was back to being in a world that didn't embrace this hair. White girls would look at me and think my hair was too greasy or that it had a funny smell. It's crazy how quickly my mood would change."

My grandmother always knew how to lift my spirits. "Oh, wow, baby girl, you look so beautiful. I love it," she would say.

I hardly acknowledged her compliments, often pretending to be tired from sitting under the dryer for so long. I wondered if it ever hurt her feelings that I was so ungrateful. There she was, dedicating her entire Saturday to driving me to the salon, paying for my hair appointments, and all I could manage was a "meh" attitude.

As I shared these childhood stories with my mother, her eyes showed a mixture of empathy, understanding, and pain. She might not have directly experienced my struggles, but she could certainly feel the emotions I had carried.

I went on to describe how, in the days following my visits to the black hair salon, I would find ways to ruin the hairstyle Ms. Gladys had so meticulously created. She had instructed me not to wash my hair for at least a week, but I couldn't handle it. How could I go more than seven days without washing my hair when all the girls around me washed theirs every night? Messy buns later became fashionable, and those were perfect after a day of not washing my hair. I blatantly disobeyed Ms. Gladys' instructions, "accidentally" getting my hair wet in the shower. My grandmother would express her disappointment, always reminding me to be more careful to protect my hair. During the summer, I was told to wear a swimming cap, but I would always let enough hair peek out to get wet in the pool. Then, an "Oh no, I guess I have to wash it" would follow. Eventually, my hairstyles never lasted the full week, and my grandmother finally gave up on taking me to the salon.

My mother carried a lot of guilt for giving me away, but I think hearing stories of Vidor had her torn. On one hand, she felt immense gratitude toward Ronnie's family for raising me with so much love. On the other hand, she couldn't help but feel sorry for me, knowing that I grew up in a place where I was unable to be myself. My mother was the only person who I truly felt safe enough to share intimate details about the outright racism that I witnessed as a child. She helped me say things out loud that brought me shame and guilt.

***

Elise looked at me with genuine sympathy in her eyes. As a black woman herself, I couldn't help but wonder if my story had offended her or led her to think less of me. Yet, there was no judgment in her expression; instead, there was understanding and compassion.

"You've not only survived but thrived through an incredibly challenging ordeal," Elise said, her voice filled with empathy. "I've heard of Vidor, but listening to your experience, I just want to reach through the screen and give you a hug."

I didn't cry the entire session, until the end. Tears welled up in my eyes, and I began to sob from a deep, emotional place.

"It was so hard!" I admitted, my voice trembling with the weight of my past.

Elise responded softly, "Being black is tough, but being black in Vidor must have been an unimaginable struggle. I'm truly sorry."

I couldn't find the words to express my gratitude and emotions, so I ended the session abruptly, disconnecting our call. I curled into a ball, tears streaming down my face. But in the aftermath of that powerful conversation, Elise sent me a homework assignment that shifted my experience. She asked me to write a letter to young Lacey, offering her the wisdom I'd gained from today's reflection. This assignment would turn out to be a pivotal step in my healing journey.

Session 5

Alcohol

Memories of my mom are always more intense when I am drink. I was halfway through my therapeutic journey, and I had this lingering desire to take a break from alcohol. If I'm honest, drinking doesn't bring out the best version of myself. At the bottom of two margaritas, there are only two outcomes – tears or arguments.

I remember my mom saying, "When you have kids one day, stop drinking. It will ruin you and them." I couldn't take her seriously, because she uttered this advice while drunk, with her daughter.

This marked the third occasion I had broached the topic of alcohol in a negative light during my sessions with Elise. So, during this session, she directly asked, "Why don't you take a break from drinking? "It was a welcomed relief to be asked that question outright.

"I'm unsure why I continue to drink," I admitted. I shared with Elise my reservations and concerns about my drinking possibly turning into a habit like my mother's.

"How did your mother's relationship with alcohol impact you?" Elise probed further.

***

Mom's drinking was usually okay. Everyone knew and loved her for being fun.

She was the life of every party, and happy hour with her was like stepping into a world of endless possibilities. We were blissful and light as the fun began. Drinks would flow, and we'd open up, learning more about each other's lives. Alcohol was how we truly connected with one another.

"I have an extremely addictive personality. I always have," Mom would often confess, her voice with a hint of nostalgia. "Alcohol, drugs, sex, food—you name it." As much as we relate the word addiction with so many negative consequences and pain, Mom was so beautiful that I almost romanticized it.

Mom was a high-functioning alcoholic. That simple statement makes me cringe. It deduces such a beautiful, complex soul to one flaw or habit that could dim her image, but I want to be truthful. She was the kind of alcoholic who kept up with her professional lifestyle in such a way that for those who didn't know her, it would be hard to guess that she had a problem. She could nail a business presentation, get blackout drunk, go to jail, and call her daughter desperate for bail, all because of a 9:00 a.m. client press conference.

In the world of public relations, my mother was a legend. An extraordinary PR executive, she navigated the industry's intricate web with grace, intellect, charisma, and unwavering determination. Her career was a testament to her brilliance, and it made her feel worthy of respect. You can imagine the embarrassment she harbored when a judge issued one of those breathalyzers to be installed in her car. She couldn't start her vehicle without blowing into this device to show sobriety. This didn't stop her from drinking, it just slowed her down.

During her probationary period, my life took me to South Beach, Miami, on a ten-week training assignment. Mom was desperate for a break and asked if she could fly out to join me for a few days. My initial hesitation was a valid but fleeting moment, as I then invited her to come out for some mother-daughter bonding time. What's the worst that could happen? I thought.

Pulling up to the arrival's lane of Miami airport in my modest Ford Focus rental car, I braced myself for her reaction. I knew that she would hate the car. Mom came out of the baggage claim exit with the allure of a movie star, turning heads with her brightly colored sheer top, white jeans, woven wedges, and fresh Brazilian blowout that she flipped with confidence as she searched for me. Her excited vacation smile turned to disgust as she pulled down her oversized sunglasses to take in a full view of this unimpressive sedan.

"You have got to be kidding me! Your company is so cheap, they gave you this maw-maw car in one of the hottest cities in the country."

I sighed and hopped out to help her with her luggage that was heavy enough for a fourteen-day trip instead of her expected four.

"Geez, what do you have in this thing?" I asked.

She got in the front seat with a grin. "Options, my girl, options."

I was always satisfied with my hotel room at the Marriott in Biscayne Bay. Of course, it was covered by my employer, so I didn't have much to complain about—until Mom came. As we walked into the hotel lobby, she couldn't resist commenting on the aging carpet, the outdated art, and the lackluster bar positioned directly past the check-in desk. I rolled my eyes and took a deep breath as we made our way to the elevators. I knew almost every staff member there and suddenly had a feeling of regret for inviting her to stay with me. Something was telling me that on this trip, her drinking might get out of hand.

Merely ten minutes later, I found myself on the phone with the front desk, requesting an upgrade. Mom insisted she'd wire me the difference, and I reluctantly agreed. Her comfort, I realized, would make the trip smoother for both of us. They had only one room left—an extravagant corner suite at an additional cost of $800 for our stay.

I shook my head and scrunched my face up to show that I didn't think it was worth it, but she grabbed the phone from me. "We'll take it! Please send the bellmen to gather our things."

Mom was recently laid off from her big-time vice-presidential role at a prominent Houston advertising agency. She had pulled money from her retirement that was already dwindling from the recession and making decisions that didn't make sense to me. Her decisions seemed erratic, a mix of fear for her future and audacious choices, like flying to Miami to critique my hotel room.

The corner room was a stark improvement. She already had the mini bar open and mixing drinks before I could situate our luggage. Mom's drink of choice was Sky vodka and Fresca—a preference that would soon rub off on me due to its low-calorie allure.

"You know I had to have my two Bloody Marys on the plane," she chimed in. "The cute stewardess gave them to me for free!"

"Mom," I reminded her gently, "I do have to work this week. I'm carpooling with my colleague Cathy, and we must be at the hospital by seven every morning. I can't afford to party too hard."

She wasn't paying attention to me. She was dancing at the window with the bay view, her cocktail in one hand and her phone in the other playing some beats that reminded me of the modern-day Lofi Chill genre.

We ordered room service for dinner, as I had a presentation and I needed to tighten up that evening. I promised her we would go out afterward. She was like a little kid, swinging her feet at the edge of the bed. She impatiently waited for me to finish and hopped up as soon as I closed my laptop.

I could tell by her demeanor, excitement, and the twinkle in her eyes that we were in for some trouble that night. My stomach was knotted a little bit and I couldn't relax. We headed to Ocean Drive to "peep the scene," and while walking, we ran into three different coworkers of mine. The massive project we were working on practically guaranteed our paths would cross with people that I knew during the night.

By now, Mom had a few drinks in and was ready to party. She was always down for dancing and couldn't resist inviting the last coworker we passed—Matt—to join us at a Latin bar. He was out with one of the other consultants for our project, and for the past ten weeks, Matt and I had worked side by side. This was our second long-term project to work together, and he lived down the street from me in downtown Kansas City. I didn't want him to be a part of the evening. I tried to wave my hand under my neck and shake my head behind my mother, but that only enticed him more.

"Sure, let's do this!" Matt enthusiastically agreed.

We were at the bar with tequila shots poured up and dancers already gearing up for a captivating show. I was smart enough to get us a taxi from the hotel, but I still wanted to stay sober enough to navigate her shenanigans. I toasted the group with an enthusiastic "Cheers" and even took my shot back with them, but as they slammed their glasses down—I spat my shot into my water cup. No one noticed, and it was a necessary precaution to ensure I could take care of her later.

Mom, in her flirtatious mood, turned her attention to Matt. "How old are you?". If I didn't act fast, I knew Matt would be her target. Matt's friend was waving down the waitress and giving the "another round" signal.

"Twenty-three, but I don't act it," Matt said.

I shot a glare at my mom as sternly as I could while trying to remain cool, "Twenty-three, Mom! He's so young."

Everyone burst out laughing at my terrible attempt to fend off my cougar mother. Before I knew it, four more tequila shots were in front of us. I didn't down mine this time, just held it to my lips. Mom was chasing her shot with a frozen margarita on the table when she noticed my sip and snatched it from me. Another shot down, and this time, she slapped the table.

My pocket vibrated; it was Cathy. I ran to the restroom to answer her call, a little panicked as to why she was calling so late. "Hey there, do you want to meet in the lounge to go over our presentation one more time? I'm feeling a little nervous about tomorrow."

Just then, the bathroom door swung open, and I didn't have time to mute the phone before the blaring music rushed in.

"Oh," she said.

"I'm sorry, I'm out tonight. I'll send you over a few notes I wrote up tonight. We'll be fine. Don't worry."

When I walked back out toward the bar, I caught a glimpse of Matt's friend talking to a random girl near the dance floor. I quickly cut my eyes to our table to see it was empty.

"Oh shit!" I scanned the room anxiously looking for my mom. No sign of her nor Matt. I ran up to his friend to ask if he had seen them, and he shook his head. I wasn't even gone that long!

I found our waitress to see if they had closed the tab out and left. She hadn't seen them either but let me know there was an upstairs dance area with a hip-hop DJ. I knew they would be there. I walked up the stairs, and as soon as I reached the top, I saw a peak of Mom's shirt through the crowd. I stood on my tippy toes to try to get a full view. There they were. Mom's hand was on the back of Matt's neck. His eyes were closed, and his hands were in her back pockets. Their tongues so far down each other's throats that I couldn't even see their eyes. I screamed. Not the quiet only-in-my-head scream. Right there, in the middle of the dance floor—with a Drake remix playing in the background, with everyone just there to bob their heads and have a good time—I screamed loudly. She turned around, only to catch me storming off. She didn't run after me; that wasn't her style. I paid our tab downstairs and called for a taxi right out front in the middle of Ocean Drive. Mom sheepishly walked out of the bar, her top button now unbuttoned, and lipstick smeared around her lips.

I didn't say a word. We got into the cab, and there wasn't a sound for several blocks. We passed another strip that looked lively, and she looked at me with a small laugh, "Care for a night cap?"

I couldn't believe her, but also knew she was serious. I asked the driver to stop and let us out at the next street. Mom began to button her shirt and freshen up her lipstick. She got out first and then only turned around after she realized I wasn't tracking behind her. I closed the door and rolled down the window as a lump formed in my throat and my eyes welled up with tears.

"Come on, Lace. One more drink!"

I had never said this before, but it rolled out as if I had wanted to for years: "I hate you."

My hand slowly reached to roll the window up. She dropped her purse and grabbed her chest, and I asked the driver to continue. As I turned my head, I saw her begin to cry.

I left her there.

Mom's drinking was usually okay. In Miami, I decided that usually was no longer okay with me.

* * *

"How do you feel about your drinking now that you reflected on this story?" Elise asked.

I wanted to quit, but it felt too hard. I have small kids and a stressful job; drinking helps me relax.

"Have you considered what your days would look like without alcohol?" Elise pitched this question just as our time was up.

After that session, I committed to a full dry year on my birthday. I decided that I would reset and prove to myself that drinking was not a necessity for me to have fun. I wanted to show myself that I could cope without a glass of wine to chase down the stress.

It wasn't easy, but Elise showed me that I wanted the change.

Session 6

Dark Thoughts

In the days leading up to my menstrual cycle, I become a different person.

I'm super sensitive and my irritability is through the roof. It's a predictable pattern, yet I somehow manage to underestimate it and allow it to catch me off guard every month.

Knowing that this session coincided with that time of the month, I braced myself for a bit of exaggerated gloominess.

"You're in bed. It must have been a rough day." Elise acknowledged as she joined our call. I had no words, so I just shook my head up and down with tears streaming down my face. I don't know what triggered it, but I was in an unshakable funk. Elise continued, "There's no rush, I'll stay right here on the line."

"My mom had such dark thoughts sometimes. I've never gone as far as she did, but I worry about it. I worry that my mind could drift to the corners that hers reached," I recalled.

"Do you have a specific memory of these dark thoughts?" Elise asked.

I pulled out a dark memory that I wanted to share out loud.

* * *

I heard her sobbing as soon as I opened the door. This was our first time living together, Mom and I, and I felt honored to have a key to her beautiful townhome. I entered slowly and walked lightly, as the sound of her cry seemed private, the type that didn't want an audience nor need for explanation.

My room was located on the lower level, while the living area, kitchen, and my mother's room were situated upstairs. To signal my presence and offer companionship, I purposefully dropped my keys into the metal bucket we kept on the console table, creating a loud sound that would assure her she wasn't alone, should she want me nearby.

"Lace!" she cried out with a tone that made me panic and rush to her aid.

I wasn't even at the top of the stairs when my eyes caught the most chilling scene I'd ever witnessed. The view forced me to clutch the railway and catch myself from falling backward from shock. The attic door, which I had never seen opened before, was hanging down from the ceiling. It looked unsteady with a rope dangling from the middle of the steps. The rope was in the form of a noose.

I snapped back to the moment, after freezing up with horror, and ran the rest of the way to reach my mother.

There she was. Seated in her favorite HÅG chair, next to the window that was cracked half-open for her cigarette smoke to escape. She had a giant sheep-like robe lazily draped around her naked body. Her big eyes were swollen, tears falling out relentlessly down her flushed cheeks. Her hair was barely hanging on by a scrunchy, and charcoal-black mascara smeared all over her face.

I dropped to my knees by her side. She was alone and she looked scared. My mind was still racing, and as much as I wanted answers or reasons, I couldn't speak. She hugged me around my neck so tightly that it almost took my breath away. Her grip was an intense, desperate embrace, and it seemed as if her pain was erupting from within her. With both hands, I gently peeled her arms away. I wanted to see her face.

I witnessed my mother crumbling and her vulnerability here on display. It was evident that she contemplated ending her life that night, and I had never seen her look so scared, so helpless, so utterly broken.

I placed both of my hands softly on her cheeks, "Mom, you're okay. I'm here. I got you." I was speaking to her like a little baby. "Shhhh," I whispered as she cupped my hands, closed her eyes, and cried more.

After I got her cleaned up and into the bed, I stayed by her side until she fell asleep. Soft lamplight illuminated her room, and I could see her brows still frowning as she drifted off. I stroked her hair away from her face and rubbed her back gently to bring her peace.

For me, however, sleep wasn't an option. I quietly slipped out of her bed and to the kitchen to clean up. "How could she be so selfish?" was my first thought as I closed the door behind me. Now that she was asleep and safe, my mind began to spin, and suddenly, I felt like that vulnerable little girl, without a mother once more. The thought that she would leave me in this world, motherless for the second time, both infuriated and shattered my heart. Even now, the memory of that attic door and the rope above my head sends shivers down my spine.

On the floor, I spotted a shattered wine glass, a detail I'd missed earlier, and two empty bottles of cabernet on the counter. Near one of the bottles, a prescription bag lay torn open, with the educational leaflet unfolded.

Suddenly, I saw a box of pills that had fallen on the barstool that was half full.

"Chantix Starter Pack," I read the label as I sat down at the kitchen table.

Mom had tried to stop smoking many times before. She told me that she tried a patch and even the cessation gum for a bit. I hadn't realized that she had started a new medication to help her to quit smoking. She wanted to break free from the habit. She hated the smell and the stigma. The feeling of being a smoker made her feel gross and inferior.

The next morning was quiet. I was up before her, making coffee, eggs, and turkey bacon—Mom despised pork. She slowly crept out of her bedroom, with the same sheep robe from the night before but, this time, tied tight across her waist. Her head was hung low and eyes to the floor, which was very unusual for her. Mom was a confident woman, one who held her head high and walked into any room with unwavering confidence. It was clear she was wrestling with feelings of shame and, now sobered, perhaps struggling to remember the granular details of the previous night.

"Did you know that a side effect of Chantix could be suicidal thoughts?" she asked, getting right to the subject.

Over the next two hours, we delved into her smoking habit and her desire to eliminate all things that felt unhealthy. In doing so, we shared our own dark thoughts and experiences. Mom was convinced that Chantix had triggered the drastic events of the previous night. Though I agreed with her, it was apparent that she needed help—not merely to quit smoking but to address her mental health.

I could no longer hold back. "Mom, I think you need therapy." I finally suggested.

Her smile was a relief; I had been apprehensive about making that recommendation, not because I doubted its necessity, but I feared her reaction.

"I do, my girl. Therapy alone won't suffice, though. I need rehab. I need more help than a single person or single pill can provide, and I can't do the work in this house or in this city."

We immediately began researching in her favorite state, California.

It took a few weeks for everything to line up, but the day eventually arrived for me to drop her off at the airport. Mom was headed to rehab, and I couldn't be prouder. I pulled into the departure lane in front of the United Airlines entrance and parked the car to assist with her luggage. She grabbed my hand before I could get out. "Thank you. Thank you. Thank you."

I knew she wasn't talking about the ride here. I squeezed her hand in return. "I'm proud of you, Mom."

* * *

I gazed back into the camera, my tone gentle, and said, "While I've never contemplated ending my own life, on that day, I was engulfed by feelings of unworthiness. The idea that my mother had contemplated leaving me again made me question whether I was enough for her or for anyone else."

Elise inquired, "Do you still harbor those feelings of unworthiness?"

I now understand that my mother's struggles and her thoughts of suicide were rooted in her own deep emotional pain, separate from our relationship. I used to intertwine her personal challenges with her role as my mother, but I've come to see the distinction.

I wish I had shown her more compassion.

I was grateful for the opportunity to share this unbelievable experience aloud. I looked at Elise and simply said, "Thank you for listening."

I had never confided in anyone about that night, and the relief of finally sharing it was liberating.

It was a scary experience, but that day in therapy — I felt safe.

Session 7

Meeting Him

At this point, I felt stuck. I wasn't sure where this next session would go. I contemplated whether there were any significant moments with my mother that remained open for discussion.

Elise skillfully guided me to connect other important issues that felt unresolved. She posed a question that jolted my memory and moved our session forward.

"Do you think it would be helpful to talk about your biological father?" Elise inquired.

How did I forget about meeting Sonny for the first time? In an instant, I recalled the forgotten encounter and couldn't help but to blurt out, "It was a complete disaster!"

***

As my mother and I both stood in the mirror, carefully applying our mascara, her hands were shaking with an uncharacteristic nervous energy. She had not seen my biological father since 1985, the day she left California in the early stages of pregnancy. I couldn't help but notice her childlike excitement to see him again, but I also knew she was still struggling to move on from the recent breakup with Charles. It annoyed me that she was getting so jazzed about seeing Sonny again.

"Mom, take it easy," I said. "Remember that he's married."

She rolled her eyes. I harbored resentment with all the anticipation leading up to this day. Mom had been coaching me for months on the significance of meeting my biological father. She framed it as a crucial step for my identity, but deep down, I sensed that this reunion was more about her, her need for closure, and her need to validate the choices she had made in her life.

Sonny was flying in from Ohio. His wife had family in Houston; therefore, he made plans to meet us one night and then see them the next. In my mind, that took a little bit of pressure from the trip.

To be completely honest, I was not looking forward to this meeting. My experience with meeting my mother was much different because I deeply yearned for a mother-daughter relationship. I had already been blessed with a phenomenal dad. To meet Sonny felt like betrayal. I felt as if I was going behind my family's back and this internal conflict filled me with a sense of worry.

I had an uneasy feeling in my stomach all day. Just as Mom and I prepared to leave, the nausea overwhelmed me, and I vomited by the front door. Her response wasn't one of sympathy but irritation, as she continued zipping up her boots, not concerned with my wellbeing. She made no effort to fetch a towel. It was evident that her own anxiety was getting the better of her. When I returned from the bathroom, I observed her in the mirror, taking deep breaths and whispering "You can do this" to herself.

I must admit that was beyond frustrating. I wanted to scream, "Get over yourself!" Instead, I cleaned up the vomit and kept my cool. Ready or not, my mother and I were walking out of the door. We met at Max's Wine Dive, an intimate restaurant with a classy southern vibe. It was only five minutes from Mom's house. The short ride was

Therapy after Mom Died

helpful, because if I had to ride across the city and listen to Mom's self-prep, I would jump out of the moving car.

We arrived early to enjoy a glass of wine, hoping it would take the edge off. I had an idea that the evening wouldn't turn out well. Earlier that day, I had informed my friend Leslie about our meetup spot, and she agreed to be on standby in case I needed backup.

We chose a table that was far enough in the back to have privacy, but close enough to be able to spot Sonny as he walked in. Our waiter approached the table with an energy that immediately made me feel good. Before I could reply to his greeting, my mother decided that she needed to set the stage for the evening.

"Okay, so here's the deal," she began, then explained the situation to him.

I was a little bit surprised, but I knew by then that she had to feel in control of every situation. The waiter's face lit up in shock and delight as he realized that I would be meeting my father for the first time. He decided that a bottle was more appropriate, and with forty-five minutes to kill, Mom and I finished the whole thing. We didn't talk much as the desperation for a buzz to get through this experience took over.

As the waiter discreetly cleared away the evidence of our prematurely initiated celebration, my father walked in. He stood at around six feet five inches, had surprisingly pale skin and broad shoulders stretching the fabric of a plaid shirt that he paired with light-colored jeans. He was chewing his gum rapidly, and he looked nervous as he approached the hostess's stand.

Mom looked at me excitedly and said, "That's him!" My response was laced with sarcasm; she had described him enough that I obviously knew that was him.

She waved one hand, his eyes locked with hers, and they both began smiling broadly. He approached our table with deliberate slowness, and by then, it seemed as if the entire establishment had been clued into the significance of our meeting. While my mother stood up and warmly embraced him, I extended my hand for a less intimate greeting. I wasn't ready for a hug.

"Nice to meet you, young lady," he said politely.

We were already tipsy, but Mom ordered another bottle of wine. Our waiter pretended it was our first. We began with small talk as the drinks started flowing, which progressed to deeper questions.

"Where did you put her through school?" and "Did you ever get married and have help raising her?"

Mom explained everything. I was mostly quiet. Not from shyness or a lack of things to say, the nerves were gone by that point. I couldn't get a word in.

"Okay, so Lacey was adopted. Do you remember the owner of the bar Michael's?" Mom asked him. Apparently, Sonny had lived in Houston for a time.

"Yeah, the one-armed white man?" he replied.

Mom admitted that he was my adoptive dad.

"But wasn't he gay?" Sonny asked. "Did he have a partner?"

The dialogue went on and on, and my ears became numb to it. How could they be so cavalier about it? That "one-armed white gay man" was my dad, and the only one I had. He picked up the slack and did the job that neither of them had done. I became increasingly upset, and my chest got tight. I excused myself from the table and made my way to the ladies' room just in time.

Once inside, I rushed to the sink and found myself to be hyperventilating. A woman came out of the first stall and immediately panicked. She asked if I was okay, and when I didn't answer, she ran out and came back with a paper bag. I clutched it tightly and used it to regulate my breathing while my tears dampened the surface. Here I was in a restaurant bathroom, with a stranger trying to calm me and rubbing my back like we were in a Lamaze class. Eventually, I managed to gain control over my breath, though my embarrassment and emotional turmoil still lingered. I let out a sigh and apologized to the kind woman. She wanted to wait with me, but I assured her that I would be fine. I pulled out my phone and texted Leslie to come pick me up. I had to get out of there.

I cracked the bathroom door and saw that both parents had their backs to me. I rushed to the kitchen and ran right through the tight space and slipped through the back door. I came out near the dumpster, and I immediately felt relief when the night air hit my face. When Leslie pulled up, I got in the front seat and sank down low. I wanted to disappear.

She grabbed my hand and asked, "Where to?"

I squeezed her hand. "Anywhere but here, sister."

I sent Mom a quick text: "Mom, I couldn't do it. I tried and it was too much. I went out the back and I'm with Leslie. Don't wait up. Tell him I'm sorry."

We arrived at a bar a few blocks down the street and spent the rest of the night ordering doubles. I numbed the feeling with liquor, and I was grateful that I made it out of that place. It wasn't that there was anything wrong with Sonny, but the two of them reminiscing and laughing about old times drove me mad. I felt like Mom had stolen my shine and I was disappointed that I didn't speak up for myself at the table.

I woke up the next morning with a hangover and the truth ringing in my ears that the night before was a disaster. I could smell coffee brewing and turkey bacon cooking from upstairs. There was no need to avoid her; I wanted to face the situation and confront her for ruining the night.

"Good morning, sunshine," Mom greeted me with my favorite cup and a big smile on her face. I squinted, confused by her cheerfulness after last night's events. She took her seat by the window, and we both took a few sips of our coffee in silence. We began to talk at the same time to break the silence and stopped abruptly. "You go ahead." I finally said.

It was clear that our moods were not aligned, and I feared the disappointment that the conversation might bring.

"So, I was planning to head to Nordstrom to return those boots from last night. They weren't that cute. Do you want to ride with me?" Mom asked.

I pressed my lips together with a short pause. "No, thanks." Without breakfast, I headed downstairs, and we left the topic untouched. It felt inconsequential, which was bizarre. How could such a momentous night be so insignificant to her? Shouldn't we have talked about it?

I eventually forged my own connection with Sonny, but it remained overshadowed by their short-lived rendezvous, creating a huge barrier that I wasn't interested in letting down. It was weird to admit it out loud, but I wasn't interested in having another dad.

* * *

"Do you think that your mother needed this meeting, just as much as you did?" Elise questioned me at the end of my story.

Just as I wanted to blurt out "This wasn't about her!" I got the point. My selfishness at the time didn't realize that my mother must have been carrying so much weight regarding my father.

I confessed to Elise, "As much as we forget it, our parents are human."

She smiled and agreed before we hung up, "Yes, they are."

I hoped that one day I would be able to give Mom and Sonny more grace, but it was clearly going to take a lot more work.

Session 8

Cancer

"I wanted to cancel my appointment today, but I didn't want that ridiculous fee."

Elise smiled through my sarcastic opening and said, "I'm glad that you didn't. It's nice to see you."

She probably says that to all her clients, but it felt good to hear it anyway.

"Are you ready to talk about your mom getting sick? You've lightly referenced it a few times, and if you're up for it—I'd like to hear about what happened to her."

***

Maci is my best friend, and her mom got sick first. Her name was Ms. Andi, and she treated me like a daughter. Ms. Andi was a constant support in my life for fifteen years. Sleepovers, volleyball games, summer vacations—she was my family. Even when I would visit home from college, her house was the place I stayed. It was a sort of refuge for me.

Andi had an aggressive cancer that she fought hard but didn't beat. She died while I was still living in the Middle East. I flew home for her funeral. I was so uncomfortable on the plane. I had taken this fourteen-hour trip several times before, but this time was awful. I followed my usual routine of a sleeping pill chased down with whatever house red wine was offered in the lounge, but it wasn't working. My eyes were puffy. I had been crying for twenty-four hours straight.

My mom stayed connected with me during my trip and urged me to take care of myself. I made plans to spend a few days with Maci and then a few days with my mom before flying back to Doha. The funeral drained me, emotionally and physically. By the time I made it to my mom's house—all I wanted to do was sleep.

I arrived late on a Sunday evening. She was lovingly waiting for me in her window seat with the television turned down low. I drug my exhausted body up the stairs and dramatically huffed all the way. There was Mom, all cozy in her robe and ready to embrace me. I collapsed in her arms. Like a baby, she rocked me, and I melted into her body while sobbing loudly. We didn't say a word. I had to be strong for everyone else all week and she let me fall apart. We both slid to the floor and were now holding each other. I slightly pulled away just to see her face, and Mom was crying too. I thought it may have been her empathizing for my pain, but her eyes told me she was hurting too.

I quickly wiped my face. "Mom! What's wrong?"

She looked down and the tears fell harder.

"I have some bad news, but we won't know anything for sure until tomorrow," she spoke.

"What's happening tomorrow?" I panicked.

"I have an appointment at ten o'clock with an oncologist."

"Wait, what?" My mind could not process the information.

"I didn't want to add my stuff with Maci's mom dying and then you needing to travel. I wanted to wait until you were home, but now

I feel so scared. You don't have to go with me tomorrow. You have been through enough."

Her going alone was not an option. I didn't have one single ounce of energy left, but I would find it. "I'm going with you." I grabbed her chin and looked her directly in the eyes. "We will do this together. It's going to be fine."

I slept in the bed with Mom that night, although neither of us got much sleep at all. We got ready for the appointment in silence. I gave a few fake smiles of reassurance, but I had a terrible feeling.

The PET scan and the oncologist confirmed that day that Mom had entered stage four lung cancer.

Mom asked, "If I do nothing, how much time do I have?"

"A few months . . . Surgery isn't an option," the doctor responded.

"If we try out radiation and chemotherapy, what are my chances?" Mom asked.

"I'd give you nine months to a year with treatment, but we can't know exactly."

My flight back to Doha was in two days, and I just found out that my mom was going to die.

I immediately went into solution mode with talks of quitting my job, moving home, and fighting this thing together.

Mom wasn't interested in treatment. It might have been the initial shock, but she was ready to ride it out without any intervention at all.

I was furious, but too tired to argue. I knew that I would be able to convince her to get treatment. I just needed to fly back and sort out my work situation. I was loyal to my company, and they paid me back in a huge way that year. They graciously let me work from Houston, knowing the time zone differences were going to be nearly impossible.

For four months, I drove Mom to treatment during the day and worked at night. I was on a strange caretaker adrenaline that was only sustainable with espresso and wine intervals.

Mom wasn't a pleasant patient. I felt that she resented me for her decision for treatment. She was bald, sick, and miserable. I had my doubts that she would beat the cancer, but I never showed it. I pushed harder than she did. I wanted her to live, and deep down, I don't think that she wanted to go on. This was her way out.

One day, as we were driving to a chemo appointment, the tension exploded. She had her window cracked just enough for her to flick and ash a cigarette. Her smoking, while I was caring for her through stage four lung cancer was a slap in the face. We were riding down the freeway in silence. I angrily peered over to watch her frail arms cross and uncross as she lifted the cigarette to her lips to take the deepest drag. I couldn't take it another second.

"How dare you?" It came out of my mouth with no control and at a volume that startled both of us. I feared her reaction. She took another puff and ignored me.

"I have put my entire life on hold to take care of you and you don't give a shit. Your smoking makes me feel like I am doing all of this for nothing."

Her silence annoyed me further, and just as I got ready to let her have it some more, I opened my mouth and she put her hand up to signal me to stop. Her face turned red, and her jaw was shaking a little bit.

"I didn't ask you to do this!" she screamed. Her words came out like knives, and it was clear that she had been holding this in for a while. "You ran back down here. You want me to live longer out of your own selfishness, and if I'm being honest, I don't think that I would have dropped everything the way that you did."

I immediately saw that she regretted that last comment, but it already stuck.

This is what I always felt to be true, that I loved her more than she loved me. My stretch for her and even my desire for her life was wider than her own.

The evening of that fight changed everything for us.

She went to bed early, as the treatment was tough that day and our harsh words were still lingering in the air.

I was sipping my last glass of red wine for the night as I caught a glimpse of my wild ponytail in the mirror. Mom's hair had always been such a huge part of her identity. Mine was more of a source of confusion, but in that moment, I thought about how hard it must be for her to be without hair.

I walked straight into the bathroom and dug underneath the cabinet to find my brother's clippers.

With red wine courage and the desire to do something bold for Mom—I shaved my head. As the strands were falling, I cried in the mirror. I cried about her words earlier that day, but I cried more because I didn't want her to die. I needed more time with her. We had a lot more fights left in us, and our time was running out.

The next morning, I walked into Mom's bedroom with my bald head. She sat up with her weak hands over her face. I slowly moved to her side of the bed as she cried and tried to catch her breath. I got on my knees and buried my head in her lap. As she rubbed my freshly shaved head and we both wept in silence, the love in the room was unbearable. I wanted her to know that I would do anything to make her feel supported and less alone.

As she wiped her tears, she whispered, "You didn't have to."

I realized that my obligation and my honor that I showed my mother was unconditional and that it came from a place deep inside of me. While she might not have done the same thing for me, I find comfort in the truth that my relationship with my mom wasn't about her or me.

I summarized this profound realization with one of my favorite poems, "In the final analysis, it is between you and God. It was never between you and them anyway."

* * *

"Mother Teresa!" Elise shouted. I couldn't believe that she caught my reference. "I love that poem and I love that you continuously chose honor for your mom. Even through the toughest days, you showed up for her in a beautiful way."

Recalling the moments of our fights, shaving my head and our relationship shift left me feeling proud and surprised. It was difficult to remember all the exhaustion and emotional hardship that came with caregiving for my mother.

"Today was so hard." I admitted.

I hugged both of my shoulders and waved goodbye to Elise. I took a deep breath and closed my laptop. I finally realized that I didn't make it this far by strength alone. My superpower is love.

SESSION 9

Her Death

"I wasn't ready for my mom to die." I blurted this truth with my voice shaking and lips quivering.

In this session, Elise graciously allowed me to begin with this raw and immediate reflection. She usually had her insightful questions to steer our conversations, but today, I felt an urgent need to dive headfirst into the depths of my pain.

My journey into therapy started in the wake of my mother's death, because it was the tipping point to so much sadness weighing on my heart. While my life's story holds many more sacred chapters, the pivotal moment that defines it all is when I walked my mother to the edge of the river. This experience crushed my soul in ways that I knew needed to be released out loud.

***

In her final days, Mom admitted her truth—she wasn't ready to die. She was scared. My mom wasn't a religious person. She grew up with a rigid Catholic routine that she despised, and that experience fueled her universe mentality over God, her crystals over scriptures, and her energy talk over prayers.

Here we were facing the end, and she wanted my help talking

to God. She didn't want to face death without knowing where her soul would go.

I thought I would find out that she was some impregnable warrior who would face death in a fearless way. I was expecting that her journey and her strength would make me feel less afraid of mortality. I was wrong. In the end, she crumbled. She was human. Outside of being my mom, she was simply a woman who was walking to the edge of her river. While I was holding her hand through this dreadful journey, I couldn't go with her to the other side.

"Facing death is the loneliest place on the planet," Mom murmured with the little bit of breath she had.

This was the first thing that she said to me as I entered her hospice room. My mom was direct in that way. Skip the small talk, let's get to the real shit.

I hadn't even put my luggage down when she hit me with this line, but she softened it by saying, "I'm glad you're here."

I inched closer to the bed and slowly put my backpack on the couch. I wheeled my worn, brown suitcase to a corner on the opposite side of the room, out of the way.

She looked so weak.

She had a hard time pulling herself up with the bed rail. She caught a glimpse of the Jack Daniels bottle I had in my hand and gave me a warm smile. She knew I would need it.

"I watched my mom take her last breath and it was the saddest moment that my heart has ever had to endure." My chest felt like it was going to explode when I confessed this to Elise, and I burst into a sob that came from somewhere deep down in my soul.

This was the moment that I had been fearing for years. I knew that if I went to therapy, I would fall apart in ways that I didn't allow or have time for in the past. Here it was—my body released a pain that I was suppressing for years.

There was a large part of my life that didn't include Mom. I have lived more of my life without a mother than with one. That is such a weird realization, and at the same time, it felt unfair. I felt cheated.

The day before Mom died, I stood in the hallway and talked to the hospice staff. "How much time does she have?" I whispered, because this question would barely come out of my mouth, and this was the only volume that I could muster up.

"The signs are there to indicate that we are in the last day or so," the nurse stated with such a gentle tone.

I didn't sink to the floor in the dramatic way that I thought this statement deserved. Everything just stopped. My body couldn't move, and no words would come up to respond. The nurse rubbed my arm slowly and said something else, but I literally couldn't hear it. I had gone deaf. I was numb and just nodded my head to signal to her that I understood.

My friend Candace slept on the fold-out couch next to Mom's bedside that night. It was an excruciating experience. The room was ice-cold, and the uncomfortable sounds that Mom made would not have been bearable alone.

I am allergic to morphine, so watching her receive it in high quantities felt unsettling. I was happy that she wasn't in pain and gasping for air, as the lung cancer had rapidly spread and gave her short painful breaths.

The next day, I was surrounded by close friends. They ushered in and out of the room to hug me, refill my cup and make sure that didn't face this experience on my own. I wouldn't have made it through her death without my friends.

At one point, we all circled around her bed and held hands for a prayer. I opened my eyes while everyone else's were closed. My friend was talking to God about bringing me peace and comfort, and I took another sip of my drink—right there in the middle of the prayer. It was wildly inappropriate though desperately needed to chase the words being spoken.

Mom's breathing became slow and shallow. It hadn't changed in a few hours, but she started to look uncomfortable. Her face would form small frowns with a wrinkled forehead and then relax after a few seconds. I asked the nurse if this was a sign of pain, but she assured me that the morphine was doing its job. I wondered if she was thinking or dreaming about regrets or life situations. Selfishly, I wondered if she was thinking about me. I can't imagine that she was at peace. Mom carried so much pain, all the way to the end.

"I just read that music may help her relax," my friend Cheri was searching for ways of comfort during the final moments on different blogs.

"It's worth a try," I said.

I crawled into the bed next to her, and Cheri started the soft music. Mom's chest started to rise and fall quickly, and her breathing changed immediately. My eyes filled with tears; she could hear it. I grabbed her hand, pressed my left cheek against it, and squeezed her firmly.

The nurse came into the room while the music played. I hadn't let go of her hand while the nurse gently checked her chest. She slowly pulled her stethoscope from her ears to her neck and looked me directly in the eyes, "It's time, my dear."

I looked around and without saying a word, my friends cleared the room. One went to go find my brother. The nurse turned the dim lights up and closed the door to allow our last moments to be private.

Damien stood on the left side of her bed, and I stood on the right. We squeezed both of her hands simultaneously and awkwardly positioned ourselves into a half slump to draw closer. I looked at my brother's face and saw anger. His lips were tightly tucked inward, and he rocked back and forth searching for an answer.

I released Mom's hand to stroke her forehead. I was trembling and my legs were giving away underneath me. I caught myself with the railing of the bed.

My brother and I leaned in at the exact same time and kissed her cheeks.

"We love you, Mom," my brother's shaky declaration poured out.

The phrase that came to my mind in these final seconds were "I forgive you," but that's not what came out. I bent down and whispered in her ear, "You were a good mom, and I am honored to be your daughter. Get your rest."

Her chest rose one last time and that was it. She was gone.

Recalling her last day to my memory and putting my pain into words immediately drained me. I felt completely wiped and I wasn't even looking into the camera anymore. Without noticing it, I had curled my legs into my chest and shifted my body towards the wall.

* * *

Elise could have stopped me. Our time was up, and I'm sure she had another client waiting, but she didn't.

When I looked back at the camera, I saw that she was crying. I wasn't sure if therapists are supposed to cry that way during a session, but it felt appropriate.

She gave me a small smile and I took a deep breath.

"I'm sorry for making you cry," I said.

"Don't apologize. You just shared the most heartbreaking moment of your life with me. I am holding onto this pain for you and with you." She wiped her face and waved goodbye.

I closed my laptop and drew in the deepest breath and just held it there. I did it. I unpacked my mom getting sick and dying. It was done and I didn't have to do it alone.

If you are reading this now – thank you, Elise.

Session 10

Our Legacy

Sharing a cry with my therapist made me feel closer to her. I suddenly didn't just see her as a container for my shit, but as a human—as a daughter herself.

I wondered about her mom. She was probably navigating her own relationship and her professionalism never served her the opportunity to share her story, at least not with me.

"Here we are, session ten. I want you to open yourself to the possibility that you may need more time. We have made incredible strides these last four months, and I don't want you to—"

I didn't let her get the full thought out before I cut in with my enthusiastic disclaimer, "This is it, our last session!"

She smiled warmly and a slight head bow of confirmation and grace.

***

"I have a daughter; her name is Ziggy. When I look at her, I often think about my mom."

I wasn't sure how I wanted to end my sessions with Elise, but it felt appropriate to find closure this way. Sharing my birth story felt like a full circle moment and I found peace in this ending.

Carrying Ziggy for nine months was much harder than my

son, Cruz. Emotionally and physically, carrying a daughter felt overwhelmingly hard.

I felt like I barely made it to the end. I was exhausted, miserable, and didn't have a single beam of the pregnancy glow or raging sex drive that I had my first round. I didn't have this much anxiety while preparing for Cruz. Sure, I was nervous as a first-time mom, but it was different.

Ziggy came with waves of anxiety. There was something unnerving about carrying a girl. I yearned for a daughter, not just to prove a point to myself, but because I craved the opportunity to show the world that I could do it right, as if that could somehow heal the wounds left by my own mother. It felt petty, but it was my truth.

After eight grueling months, something shifted with my pregnancy. Leading up to her birth, a tenderness came that final month. My irritation faded, replaced with a beautiful sense of grace and gratitude.

I remember gently rubbing my belly as the days dwindled to her arrival and constantly whispering, "Okay, sister, it's you and me. We can do this!"

The morning of her birth was calm and quiet. We made arrangements for Cruz and I took a long, warm bath—admiring what might be my last time to grow a tiny human inside of my body.

We headed to the hospital in a comfortable silence. My husband rubbed my hand, and I melted into the seat. I was already feeling a deep adoration for our daughter and ready to hold her in my arms.

There was an extremely ironic moment that happened at the hospital. One of my cousins and a dear friend arrived around the same time. They were the same two who arrived at the hospice room minutes after I got the news that my mom was in her final days.

Goosebumps surged over me, knowing they had come to usher Ziggy into this world, just as they had been there to bid Mom farewell.

I received the epidural without any issues and felt like a professional, even though I had only done this once before.

I laid back in my hospital bed and waited for the contractions to come and go. Suddenly, I felt an extreme amount of pressure. I knew this couldn't be the real deal. The nurse had just left the room and I was merely five centimeters dilated. Then again, I did request a peanut ball. It was something I saw on Instagram that new mothers were raving about. I had the peanut ball between my legs for about thirty minutes. It was magic!

"Hit the button for more pain medicine!" my cousin shouted as she saw me curl into a ball from the sharp waves of pain.

Before I could reach over, she called the nurse to come in. The nurse checked my cervix and her eyes lit up, "Whoa, it's time to push. This baby is coming right now!"

There was one thing rushing through my mind—Mom.

Tears rolled out of the corner of my eyes. My husband's face brought the tears on stronger; he was so soft with me. I wondered if he knew that I was thinking about Mom. Although he never met her, my stories kept him well acquainted with her memory.

The bright lights were now full blast with the room crowded with labor and delivery staff. I tilted my head back onto the pillow, closed my eyes tightly, and gritted my teeth. Here I was in the moment—delivering my daughter and all I could think about was Mom leaving the hospital without me when I was born. As I pushed, I cried and thought about her pain.

A weird part of me felt like Mom was in the room that day. I got a chill up my spine, which you know was numb from the epidural. I felt her there with me.

Ziggy came out on the third push without any dramatic fuss at all. They placed her into my arms, and I lost control.

I wept for her, out of gratitude.

I wept for me, out of pride.

I wept for Mom the most.

As I held my daughter in my arms, I wondered what it would be like to hand her to another family. I wondered how Mom weathered the reality that she faced that day. The papers for my adoption were finalized a month before I was born. The agreement was sealed and even if she changed her mind – my fate was written.

On that day, while I gave birth to my daughter, I experienced a deep homage for my mother. It was now my turn.

* * *

My plan was never to be in therapy long and this was our last session. While I had many things that I needed to process and sort, I had a clear goal for my ten sessions with Elise. I wanted to grieve the relationship and loss of my mother properly and effectively.

I've learned that our relationship wasn't as complicated as I put on. Yes, we had an atypical beginning, but when we got to the root of it, we both just wanted to be better for each other. Mom gave me the best version of herself, and it took the best version of me to accept that. We did the work.

I want our legacy to be generations of women who decide that the beauty and success of our family depends on intentional relationships. It all relies on our willingness to love each other without keeping score.

For Ziggy, my hope is that she leans into this relationship and everything I have to offer.

"What happens if your relationship isn't perfect?" Elise interrupted and challenged me in the moment of a utopian goal.

"That's the point." I smiled. I'm not aiming for perfection and never did with my mom.

I want the messy, the mistakes, the fights, the attitudes, and everything that can be ugly, but in that—I want her to always feel wanted.

I want my daughter to know that I choose her, I want her, and that I love her.

I glanced down at the clock. Our time was up.

I felt so much lighter and for the first time in forever, I felt free. I felt like my chest wasn't tense with the grief that I was carrying around.

"Thank you so much, Elise." I had both hands crossed over my chest and ended our time with extreme gratitude. I was going to miss her. I was proud of the emotional investment that I made into therapy.

"I'll call you when I'm ready to process the other wild parts of my life."

Elise closed our session with a beautiful smile and simply said, "I'll be here! I'm so proud of you. You did the work."

If you've been thinking about therapy, I love you—I see you. Take care of yourself, and when you are ready, help is out there.

About the Author

Meet Lacey Tezino, a dynamic entrepreneur and the visionary founder and CEO behind Passport Journeys, a groundbreaking startup. Passport Journeys is revolutionizing the world of therapy with its pioneering teletherapy app, specifically designed to nurture and strengthen the unique bond between mothers and daughters. Lacey's innovative app connects each mother-daughter duo with a licensed clinician who guides them on a transformative journey of healing and growth.

With a monthly subscription, Passport Journeys offers biweekly online therapy sessions, engaging bonding activities, thought-provoking journal prompts, and tailored communication worksheets. Lacey's vision extends beyond borders, as she plans to expand the app's reach across all fifty states and eventually into targeted international markets.

Before embarking on her entrepreneurial journey, Lacey Tezino forged a successful career as a leader in healthcare IT, with a notable tenure at Cerner/Oracle. Her dedication led her to Doha, Qatar, where she spent three years spearheading the digital transformation of clinical documentation, converting eight hospitals and twenty-three clinics from paper to electronic health records.

Lacey's impressive track record also includes serving as the Director of IT for the Menninger Clinic, one of the United States' premier psychiatric hospitals. While this may be her first book, you can be sure it won't be her last. Lacey Tezino is a visionary with a passion for innovation, determined to make a lasting impact on the world of mental health and wellness.

Made in the USA
Monee, IL
07 April 2025